IMAGES
of America

DUBUQUE
THE 20TH CENTURY

The Half Pints of Melody dally over a malt at the shop across the street from KDTH in the fall of 1941. Their weekly program was fed to the Mutual Broadcasting Company, and the boys received fan mail from coast to coast. Seated, from left to right, are: Chuck Rastatter, Chuck Serene, Joe "Kayo" Wareham, Bill Whelan, Jack Rhomberg, Jim Conner, Jack Hayes, Arthur Miller, and Louis McDonough. Standing, from left to right, are: Paul Rastatter, Bob Gribben, and Bob Link.

Cover photo: Time marches on as Dubuque's new clock moves to its new location.

IMAGES
of America

DUBUQUE

THE 20TH CENTURY

James L. Shaffer and John T. Tigges

ARCADIA
PUBLISHING

Copyright © 2000 by James L. Shaffer and John T. Tigges.
ISBN 978-1-5316-0468-4

Published by Arcadia Publishing
Charleston, South Carolina

Library of Congress Catalog Card Number: 00-106093

For all general information contact Arcadia Publishing at:
Telephone 843-853-2070
Fax 843-853-0044
E-Mail sales@arcadiapublishing.com
For customer service and orders:
Toll-Free 1-888-313-2665

Visit us on the Internet at www.arcadiapublishing.com

The Dubuque Symphony Orchestra was founded in 1907 by Professor Edward Schroeder, who conducted the group through the 1930s. His son Wendall then assumed directorial duties. Here, the orchestra is pictured in 1940. Several years later, the war created a shortage of musicians and the orchestra became defunct until 1960, when Parviz Mahmoud, Dr. Clark Stevens, Doy Baker, PhD, and John Tigges put it back together again. Mahmoud conducted the new orchestra until 1985, when he retired.

CONTENTS

The marriage of Henry Johnson and Margaret Decker was a typical Iowa marriage. Henry's father, Hans, came from Norway, and Margaret's father came from Luxembourg. Henry and Margaret were married on April 30, 1919, and celebrated their golden anniversary in 1969. They had ten children, eight of whom were living in the year 2000.

INTRODUCTION

Dubuque crossed over into the 20th century as gracefully as any town or city in the United States, beginning the year 1901 with 36,297 people. Changes were taking place in almost every field of endeavor.

Life on the farm remained a job of hard work, peace in the countryside, and the farmer being independent and his own boss. That was bound to change, however, and it did. From low prices to milk strikes and produce strikes, nothing seemed to work for the farmer, who fed not only his family and his community, but the United States and much of the world as well.

It has been stated that what was to become Loras College was the oldest college in Iowa, and that the city is home to the oldest college for women, Clarke College, which was founded in 1843.

A.A. Cooper, at the age of 81, continued to walk through his wagon/carriage factory after years of doing so, keeping in touch with his employees. When a car manufacturer approached him to change his factory from wagons to automobiles, he said "No." To him, cars were a passing fad. So much for Dubuque becoming like Detroit. Thank you, Mr. Cooper.

Dubuque did, however, have its own automobile—the Adams-Farwell—which in itself was of revolutionary design from all other "horseless carriages" of the time. Perfected by 1901, the hand-built car that had 22 coats of hand-rubbed finish applied could not compete with Henry Ford's Model T. The Adams-Farwell carried a price tag of $3,500, while the Model T, constructed on an assembly line, cost a mere $850. Today, there is one Adams-Farwell left in existence.

The Iowa Iron Works, later the Dubuque Boat and Boiler Works, built the largest working steam-driven riverboat that worked on the Mississippi River. The *Sprague* established a record by pushing 60 barges, which was equivalent to the length of four city blocks. While the pleasure cruise boat *Mississippi Queen* is a bit larger and steam powered, the *Sprague* will live on in the memory of those who know of her or saw her.

The railroads, of which four served Dubuque, slowly lost business to other forms of transportation. For example, the Milwaukee Railroad's stock sold for $105 per share around 1905. Then the railroad extended its rails to the Pacific Northwest. After the rails were laid, and electrification costs were an additional $23 million, their larder was pretty lean. Once the

Panama Canal opened in 1914, the Milwaukee was hanging on the ropes, gasping for financial air. In time, their stock plummeted to about $5 per share. Transportation soon changed, to the extent that the automobile fought for, and in time won, the majority of private transportation. In turn, trucks and buses came into their own.

When the United States entered the Great War, German Americans were harassed. It proved curious, however, that the first three soldiers from Dubuque County to give their lives for their country were Carl Heller, Peter Nauman, and Herbert Schroeder, all German Americans. Dubuque also had a Congressional Medal of Honor winner when Sergeant Matt Spautz gave his life to make certain the men in his command were safe. He was only 19 years of age. Women went to work in factories and rolled bandages, and did the same in WW II.

Dubuque became its own "state" when Iowa went dry during Prohibition, and Dubuquers flocked across the Wagon Bridge to Illinois for their gin or other illicit drinks. Since then, Dubuque, the Democratic county in the Republican state of Iowa, has been known as the "State of Dubuque."

The Ku Klux Klan made unwelcome appearances in the late 1920s, when the Klan was at its fullest strength, and again in the 1980s. However, neither amounted to much, since Dubuque would have nothing to do with bedsheet bigotry.

Dubuque in its conservatism was slow to react to the financial hell of the 1930s. There was a "Hooverville" and bread lines, but not as long in existence or length as other towns of similar size.

Dubuque has outgrown two airports. The first was Nutwood Park, site of the race track at one time; the second was located on City Island. Today's "real" airport, capable of landing jetliners, is about 4 miles south of Dubuque.

It has been said that Dubuque is a good place to raise a family. That is about as accurate and as good a compliment one can pay a town.

One

1901–1920

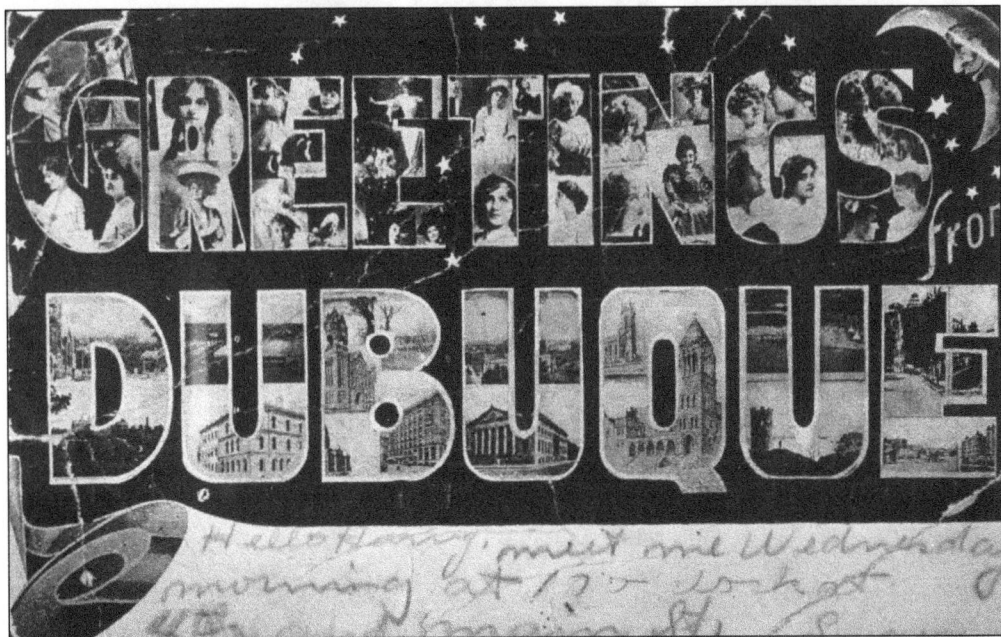

Old postcards, such as the one above, often beg questions of today's reader, such as who was Harry? Lucy? Did they meet at the appointed time at Fourth and Main Streets? Whatever! Greetings from Dubuque is the BIG message.

There was a baseball game that day, and the conductor and motorman of Trolley #79 pose next to the Chicago Great Western passenger depot, perhaps waiting for the visiting team to arrive by rail along with their fans.

Members of the First Graduating Class of Mercy School of Nursing, 1902

Members of the first graduating class of the Mercy School of Nursing are pictured here in 1902. Finley's school graduated their first class in 1900.

Mr. Richard Herrmann paying his last respects to the Late Senator W. B. [...]

Richard Herrmann arrives to pay his last respects to the late Senator William Boyd Allison. Herrmann is the man about to enter the house on Locust Street, to the right of the center tree.

This is the Country Club House, which would later become the Dubuque Golf and Country Club. According to LuAnn Goecke, the time is 1903.

When Union Electric Company's Trolley #66 jumped the track on Easter Sunday morning, 1905, prurient onlookers gathered to voice their estimates on repairs to the Diamond House.

Looking south on Main Street from the 1000 block, the above scene was captured. However, something is awry in the photograph. J.P. Buechett & Co.'s huge pocket watch points to 8:20 a.m., while the town clock's hands indicate 1:45 p.m. Hmmm…

The old church behind and across the alley from the Odd Fellows Temple was of an unknown denomination. The striking Odd Fellows Temple and the Customhouse turned Post Office complimented each other.

From this humble building of higher education and seminary, which was built by Bishop Mathias Loras in 1839, a large college named St. Joseph College was to grow. In time, St. Joseph College became Columbia College and Academy.

Additional wings had been added to St. Joseph College when this picture was taken from Prairie Street.

Union Park's beautiful fountain could be better appreciated from a distance. As a result, no one should have disobeyed the sign: New Sod, Keep Off.

A Union Electric Company crew stops to have its picture taken for posterity. The vehicle is powered by batteries, of course.

A gang of gandy dancers pose for their picture before pumping their way (in the handcar at left) to that day's job.

Jackson School on West Locust, which served the community well, is pictured here in 1907.

A pastoral scene is observed here by F.L. Egelhof in 1907. It must be spring, since the sheep have been sheared. The dairy herd stands between the flock and New Melleray Monastery's barn.

What could be more peaceful than pole fishing at Kimball's Island Park in 1907, a bit north of Dubuque? The island was in the Mississippi River.

Irving School originally stood at 2145–95 University Avenue.

The intersection of Seventh and Main Streets is here pictured looking north. While there was a scarcity of automobiles in 1907, bicycles, horses and buggies, and trolley cars still did the bulk of transporting people.

Looking south from the same vantage point shows the same to be true.

The Avenue Tap Mine originally produced lead when it opened in the 1880s. But by 1906, zinc was the main metal. The above photo dates to around 1908.

John T. Hancock established a wholesale food company in 1898. In 1908, the Western Grocer Company purchased the business. The building stands at 220 South Main Street.

The Heiberger family gathers to celebrate the 50th wedding anniversary of John Heiberger (with white beard) and his bride, the second woman to his left. The woman between them is his mother. The year is 1911.

A party is a party is a party, even as pictured here in 1911. The fiddler in the center provided the music and everyone danced.

20

When the Dubuque Shot Tower could no longer legally make shot, it was eventually used by the Standard Lumber Company, the largest lumber mill on the Mississippi, as a watch tower for fires.

On May 26, and again on May 28, 1911, fire ravaged the Standard Lumber Company, causing over $600,000 worth of loss, including the interior of the Shot Tower. Evidence of arson was discovered and a reward of $5,000 was offered, but no one ever collected.

A dandy poses with his horse and rig in 1912. He apparently was among those who believed that horses would last.

RUSTIC BAND STAND, UNION PARK, DUBUQUE, IOWA, U.S.A.

The rustic bandstand in Union Park offered many gala concerts for picnickers and families out to enjoy the park on a Sunday outing.

A pusher bi-plane with tricycle landing gear landed at Nutwood Race Track sometime in 1914. Needless to say, the audience was in awe. The first plane landed in 1909.

John Armstrong of Dubuque proved himself the "All-American Boy" when he attended the University of Dubuque in 1918. He excelled in basketball, played pro football with Jim Thorpe, and was a champion golfer. Here he is pictured in 1916 at Oklahoma City sitting in the mechanic's seat of a racing car. He was successful as a race driver as well.

Roshek's white delivery truck was gorgeous but wouldn't have had a chance against John Armstrong in a race.

A large crowd gathers at the Illinois Central passenger depot to see their sons, husbands, and boyfriends off to war. The Dubuque Yanks were comin'.

Three automobiles in the fall of 1918 gather with their owners and families to have their picture taken.

Program

HON. ALEX GRATZ, Toastmaster

America ....
Word of Welcome .... J. F. Van Vors
Address .... Rev. A. K. Walborn
Vocal Selection .... Quartette
Address .... Hon. M. C. Matthews
Address .... M. H. Czizek
Vocal Selection .... Quartette
Address .... Rev. Father H. P. Rohlmann
Star Spangled Banner ....
KOPPEL'S ORCHESTRA

Menu

TOMATO BOUILLON EN TASSE
OLD HOME STYLE

RADISHES   OLIVES   GREEN ONIONS
A LA DUBUQUE

FRIED MILK FED SPRING CHICKEN
SAUCE SOUTHERN STYLE

MASHED POTATOES   NEW JUNE PEAS

LETTUCE AND TOMATO SALAD
FRENCH DRESSING

BRICK, FRESH PEACH ICE CREAM
DEMI TASSE

CIGARETTES   CAFE NOIR   CIGARS

Our Honored Guests

Lewis Edgar Kleis	Leonard Michael Jobgen
Frank A. Fengler	Joseph William Seely
Hubert Even Myers	Henry B. Gobell
Joseph Peter Schueller	Maurice Schuman
Morris Frumkin	Bush Harry Burrichter
Otto Thomas Minges	Frank Joseph Sitterly
Walter William Jungen	Earl M. Fuller
Rudolph Beversdorf	Wilford Strawbridge Blades
Theodore Simon Scherer	Paul Matthais Kies
Frank Caleb Beckett	Bernard A. McCoy
Phillip Henry Rehder	Frank Marshall Parker
William Harry Fletcher	Henry Frank Parker
Frank Geo. Mason	Julius Carl Loosbrook
Earl Yount	Harold N. Hilbert
Frank Thill	Lester Luther
Wolf Goldstein	Andrew Vaughan
Adolph Kleith	Eugene Murray
Arthur Leniellin Barrett	Walter Louis Kuehnel
Clarence Thomas Mills	Leonard Stanley Stevens
George Knockel	Philip Julius Carpentier
Leo B. Schlueter	Hugo Westensee
Arnold William Lynch	Charles Nicolas Weber
Elwood Earl Bennett	Charles H. Luke
Raymond Frank Moore	Joseph Riedi
Arthur Joseph Walsh	Frank John Bauer
Meyer Peter Goodman	Frank Smith
Theodore Joseph Flammang	Elmer Cork Jenney
Vincent George Larkin	Frank Albert Nachtman
Henry Arnold Batteram	Jesse Oscar Caldwell

Exemption Board

J. W. McEvoy	J. J. Shae
Geo. Schaffhauser	Dr. J. R. Guthrie

Government Representative on Exemption Board
M. H. Czizek

Medical Board

Dr. W. P. Slattery	Dr. A. H. Blocklinger
Dr. B. Michel	Dr. J. A. Meshinger
Dr. H. G. Langworthy	

This is a program for a banquet at which Harry Kopple's orchestra played in September 1911.

In later years, Harry Kopple still enjoyed playing his violin. He owned and operated Kopple's Grocery Store on University Avenue for many years.

The people crowd in close to the parade at the corner of Fifth and Main Streets. While the sign hanging across the street states: "...will win the war-don't waste it," the war must be over.

The war is over! All the more reason to take the trolley car to Union Park and relax.

On July 9, 1919, weather predictions warned of possible thunderstorms in the area. No one would have guessed that a flash flood would crash into the valley where Union Park nestled.

Five people died in the sudden deluge, which caused $15,000 in damage. Restoration work began immediately.

When the University of Dubuque installed their swimming pool around 1920, it was the best facility in the city.

A ladies' gymnastic class at the University of Dubuque is pictured here around 1920.

The Telegraph-Herald moved from 7th and Main Streets to the southeast corner of 5th and Main Streets. The flag sign hanging across the street advertised Central School's show, "Bimbo," which was performed May 25th and 26th.

Engine #29, with its four-car passenger train, left Dubuque about 15 minutes before arriving in Durango, Iowa, to have its picture taken, then leaving for points west.

While the world was at war and the automobile was edging out the horse; when five people died in Union Park's flash flood; and a person could swim 12 months a year at the University of Dubuque, the one room schoolhouse continued to dominate rural education. The one pictured remained in operation until at least 1962, the year the photograph was taken. Notice the flag with 50 stars. Still, boys had not changed: never walking, always running. This picture shows the longevity of rural schools.

Two

1921–1940

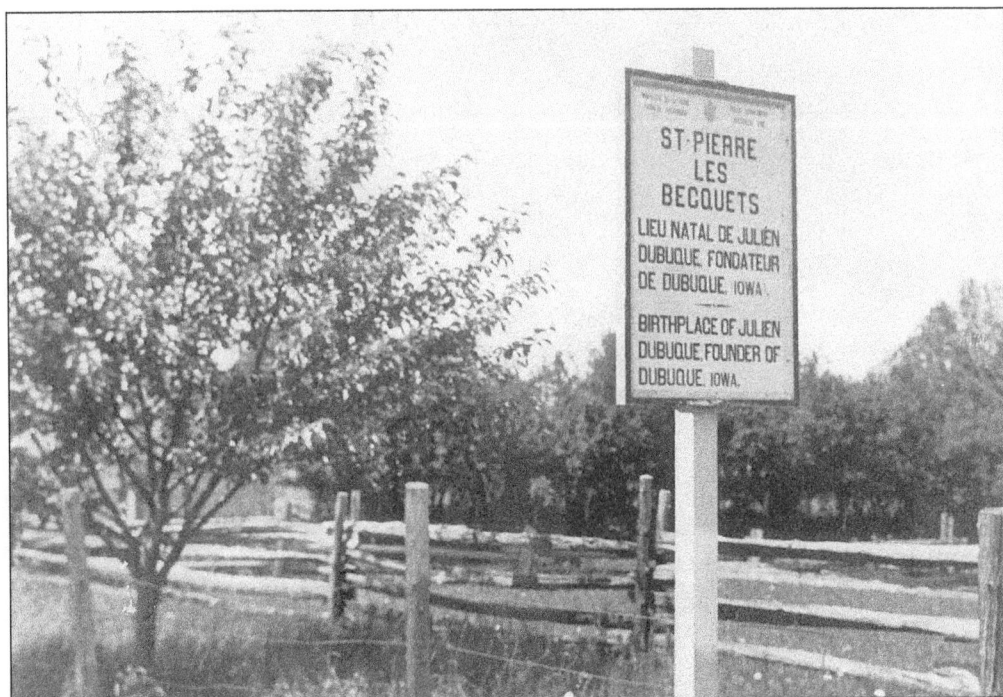

This bilingual sign is located outside St. Pierre Les Becquets in Nicolet County, Quebec, a village of around 400 people. It brags about her native son, Julien Dubuque, as the founder of Dubuque, Iowa. In reality those miners and trappers, such as the Langworthy brothers, Tom Kelly, and William Newton, founded the town and named it for Julien Dubuque.

The Dubuque and Wisconsin High Bridge opened in 1902, the end result of the company started in 1894 by Joseph Rhomberg.

The parsonage (left) was built of gray Bedford limestone in 1905, and completed as well as complemented St. Luke's United Methodist Church on the corner of 12th and Main Streets. The Romanesque buildings were begun in 1895 and the church's windows are all Tiffany stained glass. The buildings in the next block are those of St. Joseph's Girls' Academy.

With the passage of Prohibition in 1916, the Brunswick-Balke-Collendar Company converted their five-year-old building from producing bars, back bars, and other tavern furniture to producing wooden phonograph cabinets.

After a second fire on April 13, 1913, destroyed the Julien Hotel, the loss totaled $294,000. Rebuilding and fireproofing it rendered the above modern building, show here a while after its completion.

The Benjamin William Lacy Memorial Foundation in Jackson Park portrays an American Indian squaw pouring water into the pool. Lacy, who was a judge, lived in a Mansard-roofed mansion on the northwest corner of Jackson Park.

This photo looks north on Central (Clay) Street at 15th Street. In the distance the firehouse, with both sets of doors open, can be seen. Around the "s" curve (to the right) at the fire department, Central continues, but was the point where Couler Avenue began at one time. Notice the overhead wires for the trolley cars.

Established on the Emerson Estate in 1899, the Wartburg Theological Seminary has grown to rank among the largest Lutheran seminaries in the United States. The statue is of Martin Luther in this 1920s photo.

State-of-the-art in fire fighting equipment around the 1920s, hard rubber tires *et al*, poses in front of the South Grandview Avenue fire station. The station was built in 1905 or 1906.

It is 1927 and the stock market is in good shape. Business is more than good and Roshek Bros. Co. is building a new, block-long store on Locust Street between 7th and 8th Streets. When Roshek's moves into the new store, it will be Iowa's largest department store. The trolley cars' main competition, autos and trucks, are more evident.

One wonders what the two elderly gentlemen are picking up on their battery-powered radio. Could that fellow from Missouri be filling the earphones with his organ music?

The Ott Rubber Company operated for a number of years in the vicinity of the Thomas J. Mulgrew Company, which sold coal, ice, coke, and cement. Ott's was among other companies done in by the 1929 stock market crash.

Appearing to be at the "end of their ropes" in finding jobs, two men sit on a bench, contemplating their future in 1932 or 1933.

While banks had runs made on them, and some businesses closed, Dubuque remained pretty solid financially as is evident in Main Street's six hundred block by the number of shoppers, automobiles, and prosperous-appearing businesses such as Levis, Forgrave Bros. Shoe Store, Hartig's Drug Store, and Steinbach's Elite Restaurant.

Dad and the six kids pose while Mom snaps a picture before taking a ride in their apparently new "Tin Lizzie."

Saddled and ready to go, a horse swishes his tail while he studies that contraption that doesn't have a tail—and round legs?

Bell's invention invaded Dubuque in 1876, but it wasn't until the '20s and '30s that rural America slowly received telephone service.

Trolley cars have a few years of service left to perform before the unthinkable effort of stopping the service and pulling up tracks takes place.

Before the installation of traffic lights, police officers directed traffic.

It's been dry for a while and there should not be any chance of getting stuck in the mud. It took Iowa until the '30s to "get out of the mud."

Here's an ordinary home in an ordinary neighborhood. A hitching post stands in front for those still using a horse and buggy, whose use by some lasted until the late '30s. Either an ivy or grape-vine arbor provides shade at the back of the house.

The intersection of 20th Street and Central Avenue is shown here in the early '30s. Ragatz Drug Store was a fascinating place where a person could shop for all sorts of things. Next door, to the right, the Busy Bee Cafe has yet to acquire its unique buzzing-bees-flitting-around-a-beehive neon sign.

The farmer's' market, which surrounded City Hall, continued with horses and wagons into the automotive era. As late as 1940, one elderly woman went to market with her horse and buggy to sell her produce.

The theatre at Union Park offered many forms of entertainment. It was destroyed in the flash flood of 1919.

A deathly stillness must have held Union Park a few days after the flood, while curiosity seekers walked among the ruins.

Union Park was rebuilt but was never successful again. The new owner, Interstate Power Company, announced that Union Park would close. Automobiles and Eagle Point Park had taken their toll. The dance hall had replaced the theatre.

The dance hall and floor were bought and moved to a location north of the former race track and city airport, Nutwood Park, which had moved to City Island in 1933. Melody Mill hosted just about every big band in the country.

This is the entrance to one of the most beautiful, scenic city parks in the United States.

Three states—Iowa (right), Wisconsin (left), and Illinois (straight ahead)—are viewed from Dubuque's Eagle Point Park.

Pools, rock gardens, Indian Council Circles, and Frank Lloyd Wright-influenced buildings came to Eagle Point through the W.P.A. projects of President Roosevelt. When he visited the park he called it "quite a boondoggle." Maybe he didn't know the meaning of the word. Then again, maybe he did.

A Memorial Day Parade is witnessed by the Palace Theatre, formerly the Dreamland Theatre, and Roehl Phillips Furniture Store (on the right) and Renier's Music Store, Herrmann's Furniture, and Fosselman's Jewelry Store (on the left) in the 500 block of Main Street.

The Princess Theatre is shown here the way it looked shortly after completion.

Roger Broessel sits in the cab of his home-built truck. The other kids and Roger made up one of the good north-end "gangs" that had wonderful summer vacations from school.

The Federal Bank Building is completed and in operation. The American Trust, one of the Dubuque banks that survived the Great Depression, did business in the Bank and Insurance Building. The two institutions operated across Ninth Street from each other. The Princess Theatre was next to the Federal Bank Building.

Colonels John Tigges and Bert Hendricks were two of the best auctioneers in the '30s. In February, 1937, they cried 34 farm auctions without working a single Sunday. Some days they held three auctions, each taking a small one in the morning and joining forces for a larger one in the afternoon.

Two children pose in front of a float for the 1938 centennial celebration of Iowa's inception as a Territory.

The Dubuque Business Men's Club House was taken over by the Dubuque Chamber of Commerce.

"Buy me some peanuts and Cracker Jacks..." This is the old ball park on the 4th Street Extension.

Here is a more familiar view to the fan: the outfield, the Shot Tower, the Dubuque Star Brewery (Iowa's last brewery, pictured at right), the billboard fence, and the Wisconsin Hills across the Mississippi River in the background.

50

Mahouts guide their circus elephants past S.S. Kresege's Five and Dime Store at 8th and Main Streets, heading north toward Melody Mill's grounds where the circus will be held.

Ray Clemens Motor Sales is promoting the 1939 Graham automobile at the dealership, located at 403 Iowa Street. Unfortunately, the car's manufacture was stopped. Notice the beautiful, albeit dirty, Ford in the foreground and the Federal Highway 52 marker on the light pole.

In 1939, Bishop Mathias Loras, who founded St. Raphael's Academy and Seminary in 1839, was honored by having Columbia College and Academy (formerly St. Joseph's College) renamed Loras College and Academy. A larger-than-life statue of Bishop Loras was unveiled the same day.

1940 would prove to be the last peaceful Christmas season in the United States for the next four years. Such tags were made by Denison's.

Three

1941–1960

Toll House, Julien Dubuque Bridge

Here is an "official" portrait of the recently completed, prize-winning Julien Dubuque Bridge. Begun in April of 1941, and finished in August 1943, it was paid for by tolls. It became toll-free in December 1954.

Dubuque loved to promote itself with such cards as this one. And "whoop it up" they did with circuses, carnivals, huge church picnics, and parades.

Bob Gribben, who would one day precede Dick Clark with "teen hops" in Dubuque, is decked out in a choir boy's surplice, collar, bow, and cassock. He was also one of the Dubuque pre-teens who sang coast-to-coast from KDTH in 1942.

The Reverend Chaplain Aloysius Schmitt, who attended Loras College and was ordained a priest four years later, served at St. Mary's Church in Dubuque. After joining the Navy, he was assigned to the *U.S.S. Oklahoma* and died at Pearl Harbor, the first chaplain to give his life in WW II.

While war raged around most of the world, the Trappist Monks at New Melleray Monastery prayed for peace at their prayer gatherings and daily mass.

RATION STAMP NO. 29	RATION STAMP NO. 30	RATION STAMP NO. 31	RATION STAMP NO. 32
RATION STAMP NO. 33	RATION STAMP NO. 34	RATION STAMP NO. 35	RATION STAMP NO. 36
RATION STAMP NO. 37	RATION STAMP NO. 38	RATION STAMP NO. 39	RATION STAMP NO. 40
RATION STAMP NO. 41	RATION STAMP NO. 42	RATION STAMP NO. 43	RATION STAMP NO. 44
RATION STAMP NO. 45	RATION STAMP NO. 46	RATION STAMP NO. 47	RATION STAMP NO. 48

Everything worthwhile was rationed during WW II: gasoline, which helped preserve everyone's tires; sugar; coffee; and tires. Fresh fruit and vegetables were rare out of season, and people planted victory gardens and canned their own produce.

It seems there's one in every barrel. Frederick W. Kaltenbach bought Adolph Hitler's philosophy and moved to Germany where, as a member of the Nazi Party, he broadcast propaganda to America. He often mentioned former friends in Dubuque by name. He was taken prisoner by the Soviets and allegedly died while a Russian prisoner of war.

After flying 50 successful B-17 missions over Germany, Lieutenant Robert Breitbach was reassigned to training B-17 crews in the United States While on a training mission, he flew over Dubuque's "North End" to show the trainees where he grew up, went to school, and where his girlfriend lived. Flying at 500 feet, his B-17 developed engine problems and the plane crashed, killing all on board, a few miles south and west of Dubuque. Lieutenant Breitbach was buried with full military honors after a funeral mass at his home parish, Holy Ghost Church.

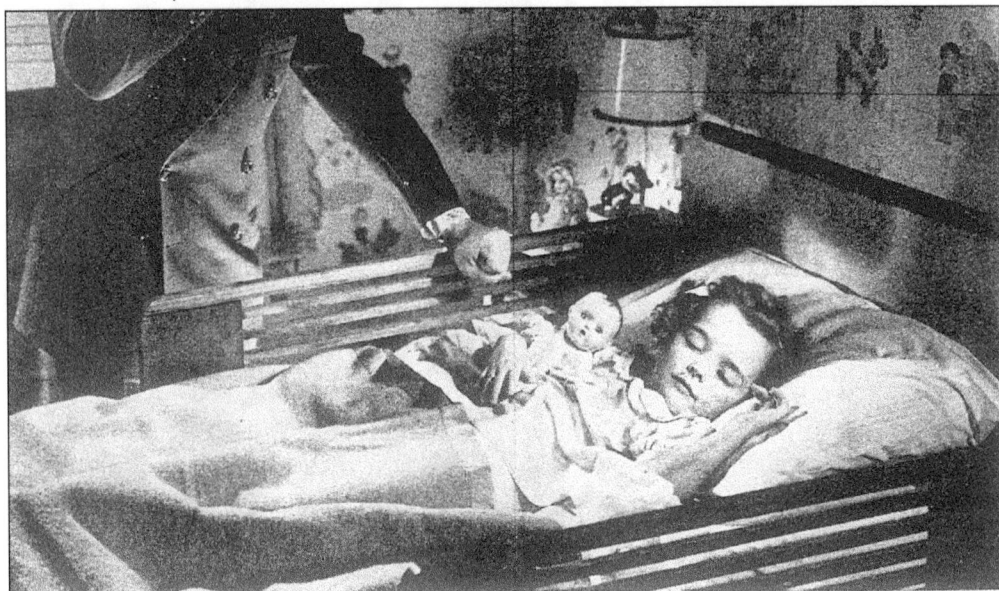

the very thing we're fighting for!

Depictions of the effects of war were everywhere during WW II. The caption of the artwork above says it all.

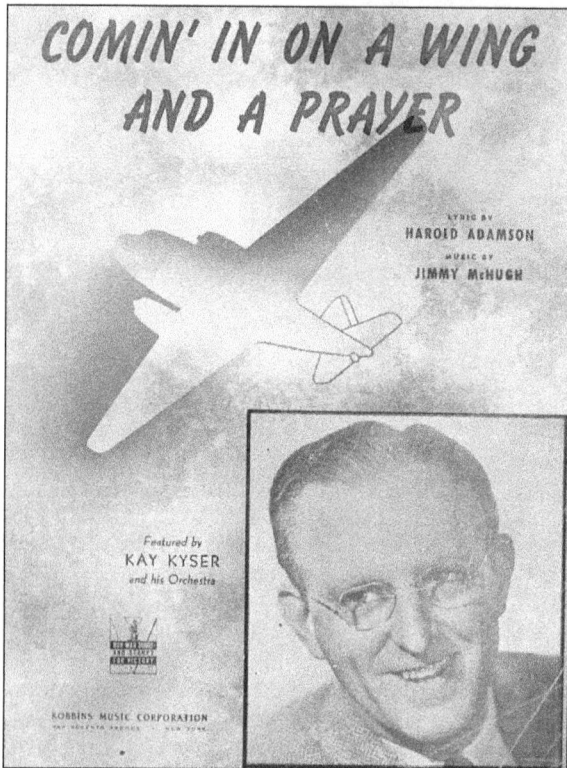

"Coming In On a Wing and a Prayer" was inspired by shot-up bombers that barely made it back to England after bombing Germany.

"Bell Bottom Trousers" was a light-hearted salute to the United States Navy. Songs such as this one kept spirits up in the folks at home as well as those in service.

Irving Berlin's "This is the Army" was all too often a grim reminder to the foot soldier that no matter what, there were orders to obey and objectives to be accomplished.

Everywhere a person looked during World War II, reminders to "Buy War Bonds" could be seen. The Minute Man was the symbol for fighting the enemy, even from home.

Father Albert Hoffman, the most decorated Army Chaplain of World War II, lost a leg at the front. He resumed his normal duties in the Dubuque Archdiocese after the war.

Paul Howard, still in uniform and home on furlough, visits with co-workers. They are, from left to right: Howard Hammerand (behind Paul), Ray Unmacht, Charlie Young (in vest), Fred Leute (under 1945 calendar), Bill McFarland (looking at Paul) and Charlie Stevens, who is working.

STAIRWAY LEADING TO MADISON PARK
AT 17TH AND MAIN STS.,
DUBUQUE, IA.—14

By 1945, these architectural steps were showing signs of wear. Installed in 1918, this set proved more durable than the wooden steps of the 19th century. Ornately designed and lighted, the eight flights of steps included a spiral staircase and shrubbery pots.

The Dubuque Water Works on Rhomberg Avenue is pictured here, before the new plant was built.

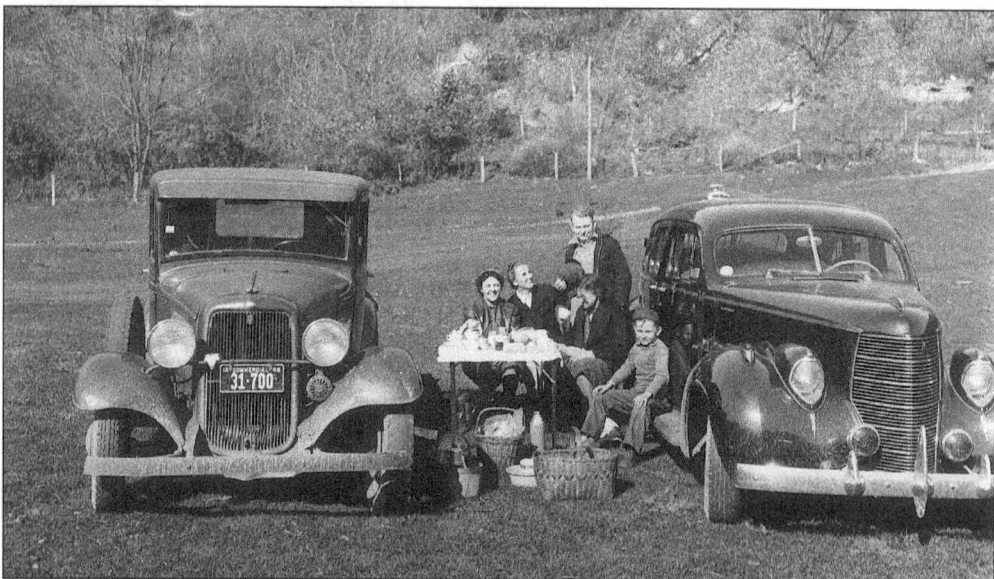

Knowing that gas and tires were available in 1946 prompted the people above to go on a picnic. The Ford pickup survived and the Studebaker Sedan appears in mint condition.

Kretz Cafeteria took over the building at 598 Main, which prior to 1929 housed the Second National Bank.

The Twin Cities *Zephyrs* pass each other on the east bank of the Mississippi River, a bit north of Dubuque and East Dubuque. The year is late 1945 or early '46. The silver diesels, E-7s, were acquired in late '45 and complemented the stainless steel trains.

The Clydesdales from the Anheuser-Busch Brewery in St. Louis, Missouri, visit Dubuque and pose with an unidentified woman at 24th Street and Central Avenue.

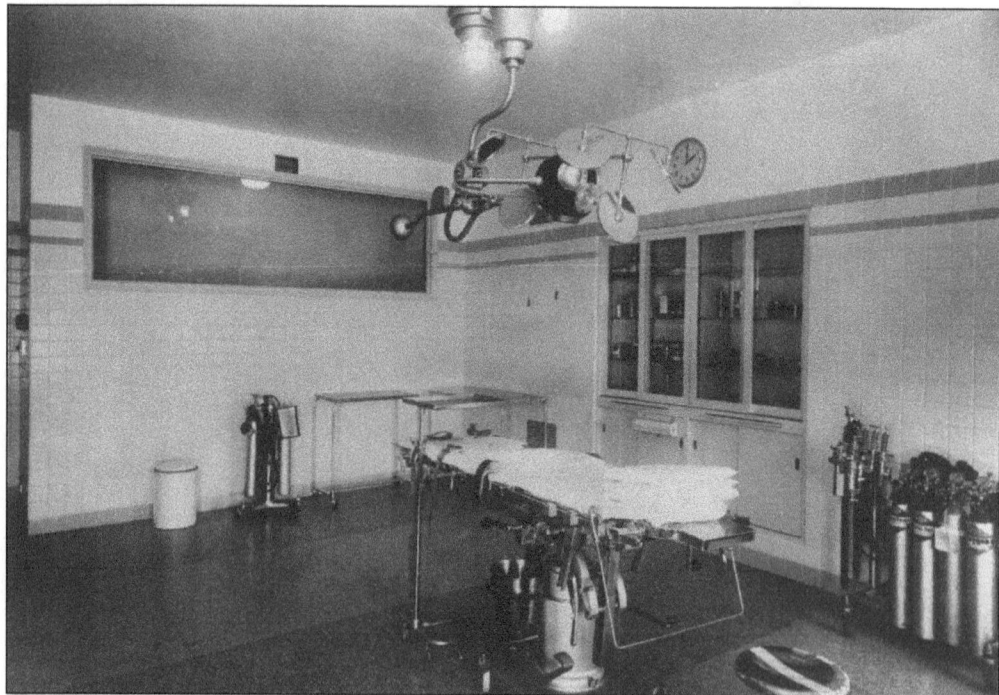

St. Joseph Mercy Hospital began expanding in 1947. Here, an operating room waits, at 2:00 a.m. or 2:00 p.m., to be of service.

Any south-ender from "Little Dublin" over the age of 50 would remember the elaborate coaling towers on the Illinois Central Railroad property, which was skirted by the Milwaukee Road. This photo dates to around 1948 or 1949.

Here is a view of Utzig's Shoe Store in the 1000 block of Main Street. Arnie Utzig also served as a state legislator for a number of years.

Dubuque, in the 1940s and 50s, had at least 18 passenger trains available to head north, south, east, or west, including the Chicago Great Western's "dinky."

A trip downtown was useless unless a bag of Browne's popcorn was included.

Surely those girls can't be headed for the Avon, formerly the Princess, without a bag of Browne's popcorn. That double feature won't be nearly as good without popcorn. They're crossing the 800 block of Main Street on a rainy afternoon in the early '50s.

Radio Station WDBQ AM-FM operated out of the second floor of the First National Bank Building. While the bank won't open for 20 minutes, rest assured the announcer is at the mike. Next door Hingtgen Wallpaper and Paint Company has moved out.

The interior of the Dubuque County Jail was designed by John Francis Rague. It was not a nice place to be incarcerated.

Everybody loves a parade. This one has drawn a good-sized crowd. On the right, just beyond the traffic light, is the one-time-bus-turned-perma-stoned popcorn stand. The small building beyond it is the former Swiss Sandwich Shoppe, where the 15¢ hamburgers were fantastic. It is currently Mellon's Sandwich Shop.

The city lost a great restaurant when the Chateau burned. But, like the phoenix, it rose from the ashes to become The Chateau Supper Club and Motel.

It's 1957 and D-X gasoline has introduced its new additive, Boron. Hall's D-X at 960 Dodge is doing a great business, especially since the price per gallon is only $.359. The 12.8 gallons cost $4.60 and should get the A-1 Moving Service station wagon home without stopping for gas.

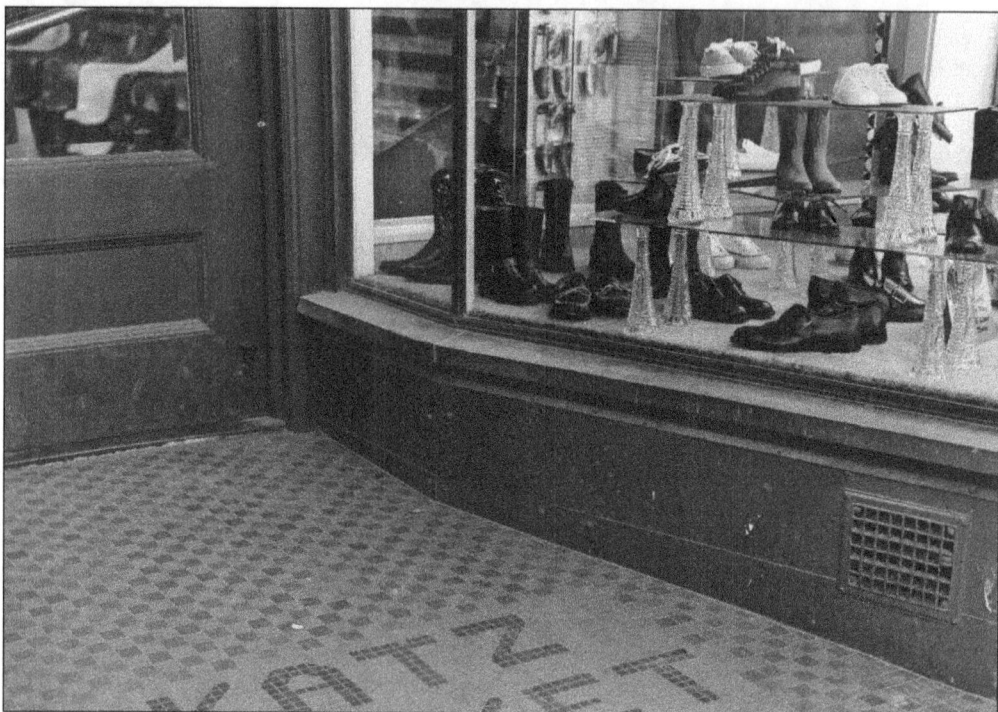

Katz's Market operated across from the Second National Bank. While the tile entryway of Katz's remains, notice that shoes are sold in the store instead.

Molo Oil Company served Dubuque with Sinclair Products for many years at gas stations, most of which offered full-time mechanic services as well as home fuel oil delivery.

Two modes of public transportation happen to meet in East Dubuque at the turnaround near the Burlington Depot, or it might be close to train time. The man-made rock formation on the right above the parked car is the Illinois Central Railroad tunnel that leads to the bridge across the Mississippi to Dubuque.

Time is flying for Dubuque and the sidewalks and curbs are looking a mite tacky. Renier's music store has moved to the east side of Main Street and three knee-socked girls stand under the awning planning what to do next.

Jaeger Hardware Store has expanded into an empty store. Notice the steps on the right, which lead to a different level.

This is the exterior of Jaeger Hardware. The small store, in front of and to the left of Cobb Optical Company, is the new addition in the upper picture.

Like most river towns, Dubuque's downtown is appearing a bit tired. Perhaps it needs a shot of "something" to bring it back to life.

Ever wonder what made the two cars on the world's shortest and steepest railway work? An electric motor operated from this room. Notice the ticket window on the right.

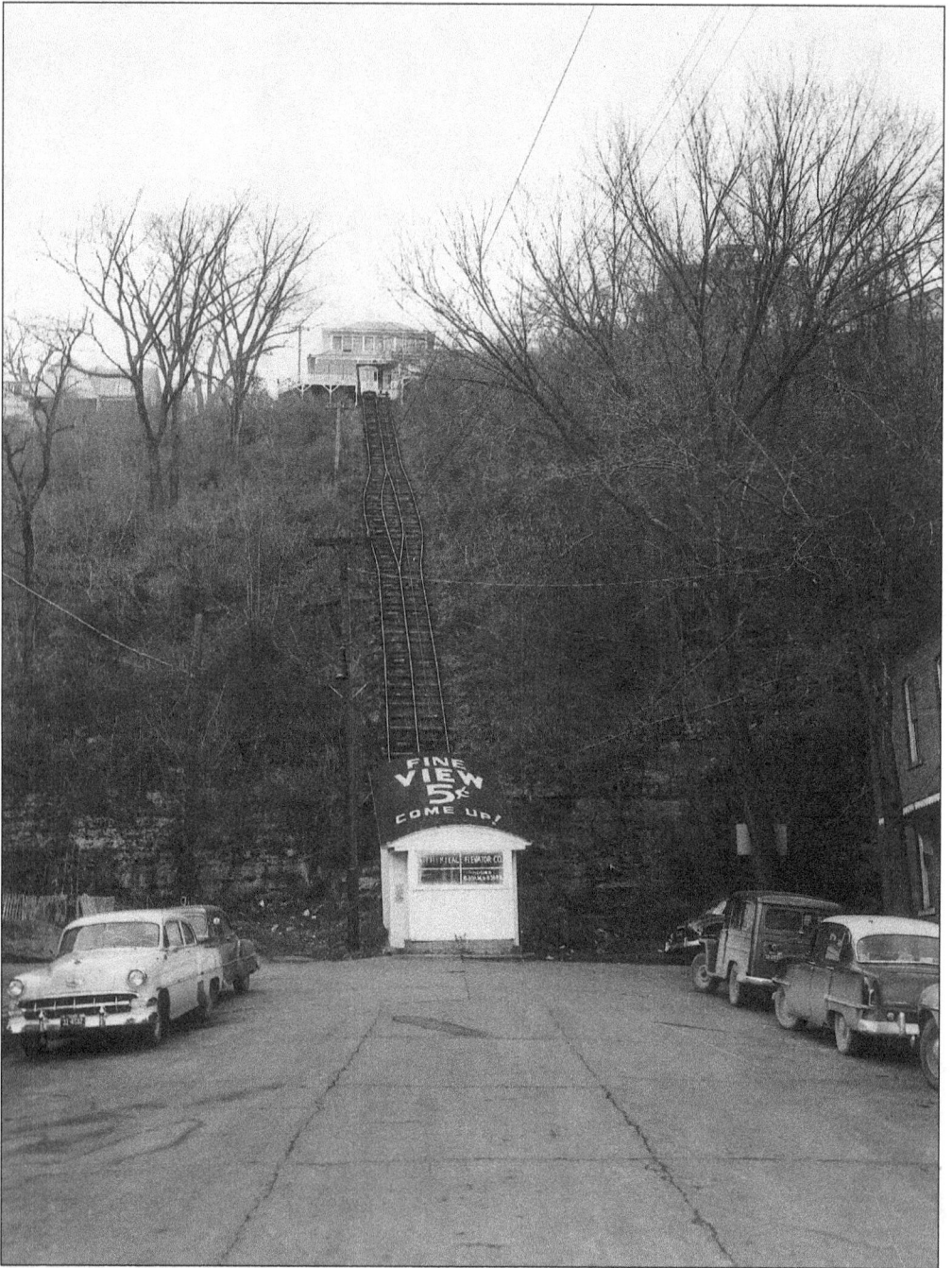

The fare was 5¢ from the first, when J.K. Graves conceived the idea for this funicular railway. Get in, pull the cord and sit down. In seconds you're at the top—or bottom.

Main at 11th Street was the beginning of the north end of downtown Dubuque's shopping area. Holscher's Apothecary, Schlueter Insurance, and Hruska Photographer were the last businesses. A movie theatre and a former service station-turned-Kaiser Frazer showroom/dealership, present in the late 1940s, were gone when this picture was taken. The Medical Associates Clinic and a neighborhood bar were the only other businesses.

Police officer George Schlegel, the "mayor" of 8th & Main Streets, appears to be focusing in on someone or something. There are shoppers galore, and stores—even more. From Hartig's Rexall to a pizza shop, a finance company to a jeweler, the Big Shoe Store to Zuckie's Ladies Wear, Leath Furniture and Roehl Phillips Furniture, Tranel's Cafeteria...They're all there plus many more.

The Facade Building, which housed Spensley and Gallogly Insurance Agency, the M & Z , an orthopedic shoe store, plus others, will eventually fall to clear the land for American Trust and Savings Bank's parking lot.

While the Facade Building was being demolished, it appeared as if Key West, a tiny town south and bit west of Dubuque, was in for some changes as well. Notice the mileage signs beyond the surveyors. Dubuque's third municipal airport and the road to Maquoketa are to the left on Highway 61, while Highway 151 goes to the right, taking motorists to Anamosa and Cedar Rapids, Iowa.

Four

1961–1980

If a person looks closely at things he or she passes every day, art can be found in nature, buildings, and even in a fence, as in the example shown above.

GM Bus number 318 was assigned by the Interstate Power dispatcher to the Main route. The trolley cars were much cleaner, leaving no diesel exhaust in their wake. They were a lot quieter, too.

An experiment using a scatter light ended after a fair trial. Each street got its turn to move, and when all the traffic was brought to a halt, the pedestrians could cross in any direction they chose. While there are two Laury Walgreen Agency Drug Store signs, the store was L-shaped and had two entrances, wrapping around the Hat Box and the United Cigar Store.

Tranel's Cafeteria, formerly Kretz's Cafeteria, did more business at 598 Main Street than did the Second National Bank. Notice that a lot of the buildings have retained their 19th century appearance, despite gaudy designs and some "modern" facades.

The Page Hotel catered to rail-passenger traveling salesmen for years, since the Milwaukee Road depot is just to the left of the blinker-crossing signal. The sign states: "Best Food in Town," and that was no mere boast.

The Julien Hotel's main lobby is shown the way it appeared August 28, 1962, shortly before the new owner, New York architect Louis Pfohl, completely renovated the hotel to become the Julien Inn.

Frommelt Awning Co. had already moved in 1962, when this picture was taken, to new facilities on Huff Street. The Onyx Restaurant was next door to the Julien Inn.

When the Chicago, Burlington, and Quincy Railroad's #5632 steam locomotive came to town October 1, 1963, many people rode the excursion train from Dubuque to Savanna, Illinois, and back. Those who didn't stood in awe of the mighty Iron Horse. Some waxed nostalgic about the past, while some saw a steam engine for the first time and were fascinated by the sight.

On February 6, 1961, the University Civic Symphony Orchestra, under the auspices of a board of directors and the baton of Parviz Mahmoud, presented its first concert at Dubuque Senior High School. Stuart Canin was the violin soloist and performed Wieniawski's 2nd Violin Concerto. In time, the orchestra's name was changed to The Dubuque Symphony Orchestra, which is Iowa's oldest orchestra, founded in 1907.

This is St. Joseph Mercy Hospital as it appeared in the '60s. The older section to the right is most of the third hospital built by Mercy. The rectangular building right above it is the student nurses' dormitory . The newest hospital was constructed in a cruciform shape, and the older five-story building is St. Anthony's Home for the Aged.

Here is the view upon entering the new "old" ball park on the Fourth Street Extension. It was the work of one man, Johnny Petrakis, for whom the park was named. He was voted minor league executive of 1961, when he drew in more attendees than any other Class D Club.

The Dubuque Women's Club held an annual art festival and picket fence sale for many years.

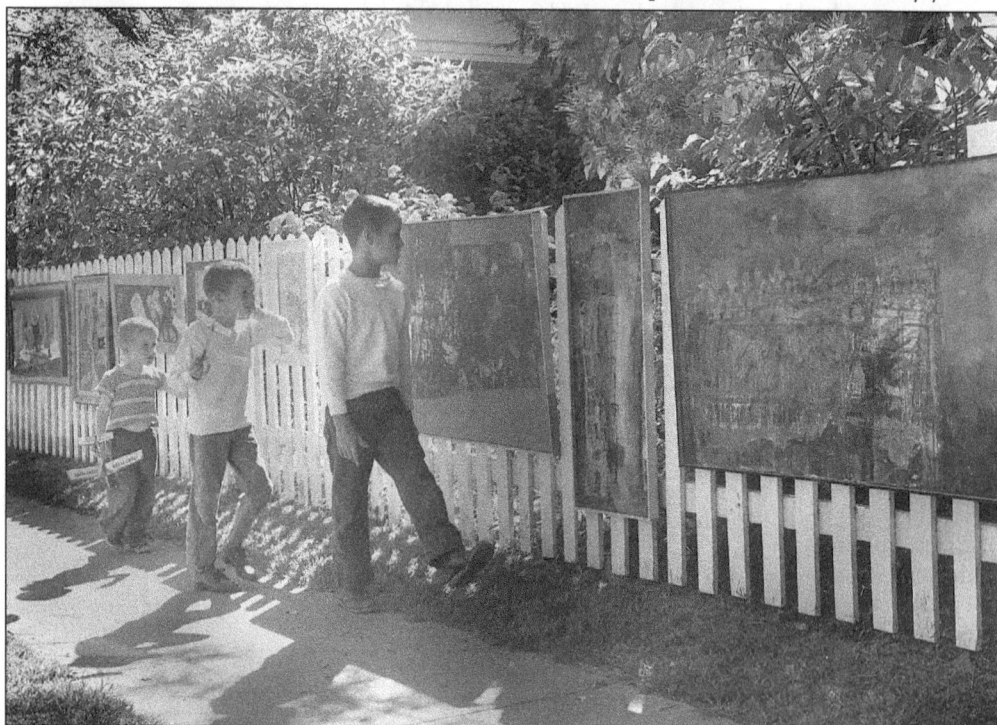

Art that was hung on neighbor's picket fences attracted the younger set as well. Above are two balsa-wood glider pilots, and someone who appears to be doing the goose step while enjoying the offerings of different artists.

The "old" Central Fire House became known as the Ninth Street Station, and has existed from horse-drawn equipment through modern fire fighting trucks.

The interior of the Ninth Street Station shows the equipment polished and ready to go, from the hook and ladder on the left to two hose trucks and the chief's car, parked in front of the middle truck.

The first floor of Roshek's Department Store, at one time Iowa's largest, is shown here. Pictured is one of the many ladies' departments. The light is off to prevent glare for the photographer, James L. Shaffer.

The Lincoln Block housed Bayless Business College for over a century. Bartels and McMahan Engineers and Surveyors occupied offices on the second floor. This photo dates to the 1960s.

J.C. Penny Company virtually built a new store with a modern front that complemented the style of Tradehome Shoes. The Bank and Insurance Building's name was changed to the Fischer Building and an extra floor was added along with a bit of modernization to the first two floors. Business is good: look at the cars and shoppers.

Feltes' Motor Company Inc., sold HiGrade Used Cars, not pre-driven vehicles.

The Grand Tap at the corner of 8th and Iowa Streets featured Dubuque Star Beer along with Hamm's Beer and Holiday Beer. Next door and out of the picture, Syl Lambert operated a tire vulcanizing business. Why hasn't that curb been repaired? Something is going on.

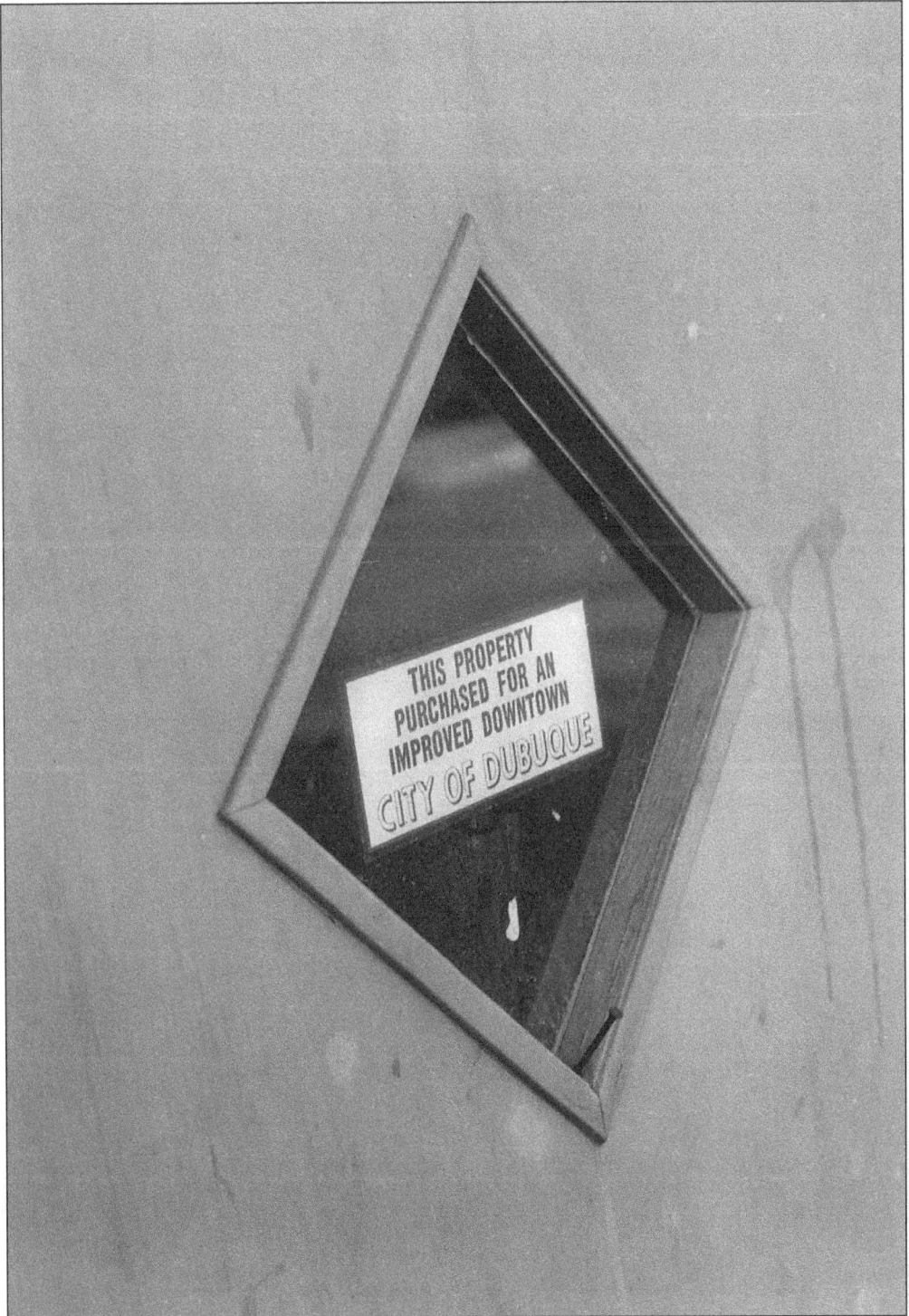

The something that was going on was urban renewal. Signs, like the one above, began showing up all over the downtown area. Sprayed numbers were applied to buildings which would be demolished.

Matt's 8th Avenue Restaurant at one time had a huge Hammond organ in the far left-hand window facing the tables. The restaurant began humbly as a Maid-Rite Sandwich Shop years before. Now, it was doomed.

Shike-Richardson, Inc.'s building is also doomed, and the dealership will move to the west side of Dubuque.

The Diamond Block, with its twin peaks and gargoyles, was built in 1887 and would be torn down along with the rest of the block. The apartments are vacant, and similarly, the businesses have moved out, except for the Tropics Lounge, which accounts for the parked autos.

Even fewer cars and only one pedestrian can be seen here. Notice that the old First National Bank Building is gone, as is the building across Fifth Street.

A photo of the block north of the prior two photos shows even fewer cars, and one man about to walk under Tranel's Cafeteria marquee-type sign. Is downtown becoming a ghost town?

The intersection of Eighth and Main Streets is recorded here, looking toward the former Roshek Bros. Department Store and Montgomery Ward Department Store. Both have moved to Kennedy Mall on the west side of Dubuque. However, that block of buildings will be saved, along with the drugstore and shoe store. Dirt streets with wooden bridges allow pedestrians, few that they are, to move about. The Kresge Store ceased operations. Most shoppers were on the west side in stores such as the K-Mart, Roshek's, and Wards.

A lone shopper makes her solitary way south along what used to be Main Street.

This photo looks north on Main Street from the south end of the 800 block, while a woman and her dog walk past shops that are still operating and open for business.

The Goodyear Tire dealership was among those that migrated to the west side of Dubuque.

Of all the businesses in the 700 block of Main, only Walkers Shoe Store and Hartig's Drug Store stayed. The latter moved into the Osco Drug Store location.

Looking east on Eighth Street, The Grand Theatre, currently a movie theatre, has a bright future. The rest of the up-close buildings remain mostly as office buildings.

Allied Camera Center stayed longer than most before moving. The building on the right remained, as did the two on the left.

Everywhere one looked, one would see equipment and men working, trying to "make a silk purse out of a sow's ear." These new projects were undertaken to improve downtown Dubuque.

This view looks north on Iowa Street, which intersects with Ninth Street. The fire station building is still there, but the department will move one block east into new facilities on Ninth. We can see that concrete has been poured. There's light at the end of the tunnel, after all.

A lonely man walks toward the camera. Half hidden in the shadows, could it be...

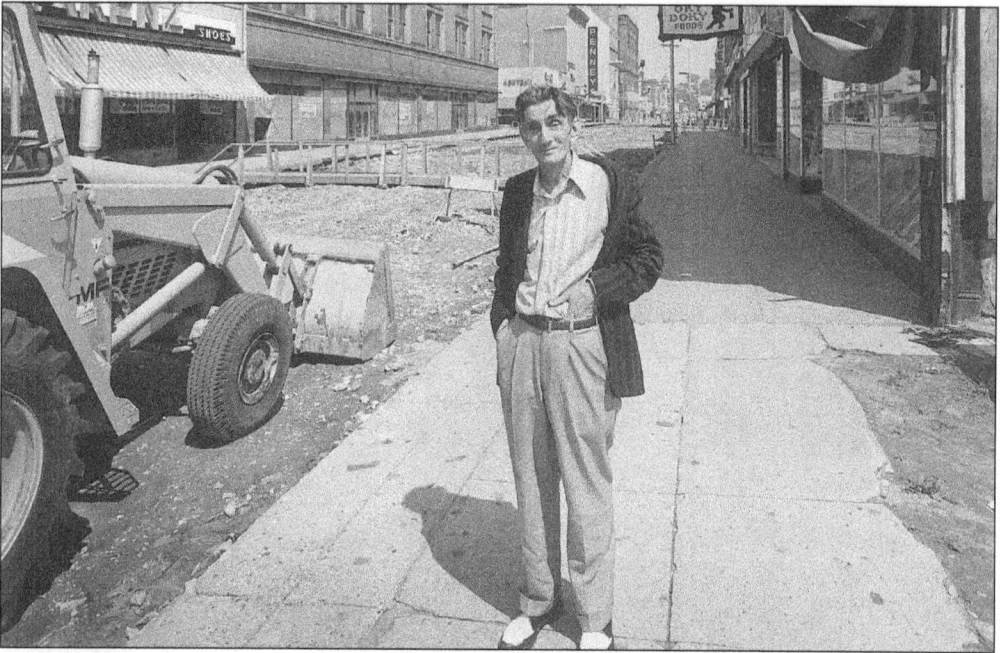

Of course, who else but Dubuquer Damon Runyan's character "Muzzy" Scardino? "Muzzy" knew practically everyone who came downtown. He was a gambler at heart and when he couldn't find a game, he made "deliveries" for various people. Could "Muzzy" have inspired Al Bundy's hand-in-pants character on TV's "Married With Children?"

Here is City Island in June 1979, the one-time home to Dubuque's second airport. During WW II, a four-engined B-24 Liberator bomber had problems and landed between the two roads. Most of the trees weren't there at the time. The plane was dismantled and shipped out on the Milwaukee Road. The first stock car track followed and today the Dubuque Greyhound Park occupies a good deal of the island, along with a park.

The William C. Brown Publishing Company outgrew its previous place of business on South Locust and moved into the beautiful building in the photo, located in the Industrial Park near Lake Peosta, which is separated from the Mississippi River by Chaplain Schmitt Island.

Taken down from its location above the Tradehome Shoe Store, the town clock was renovated inside and out before being hauled piecemeal to its new location...

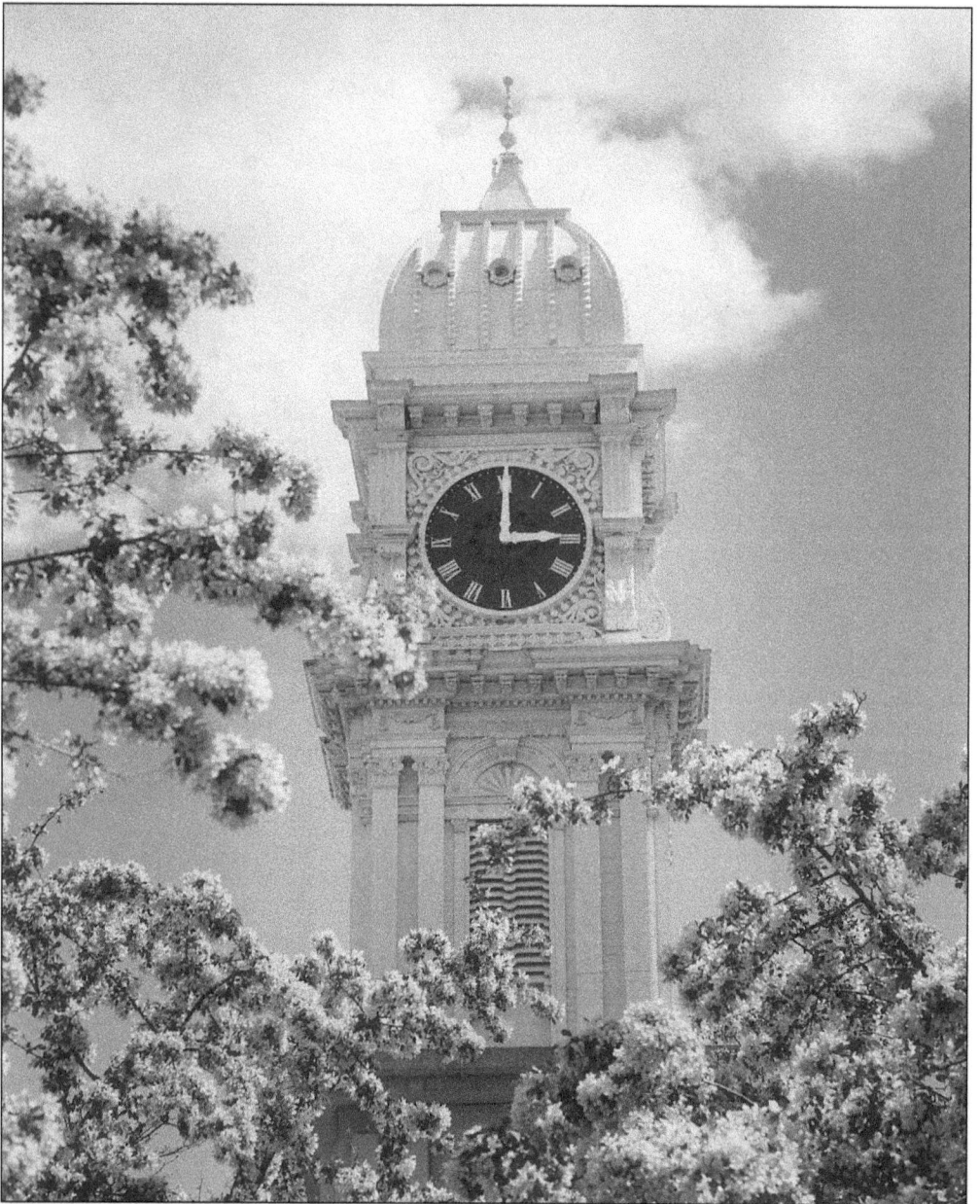

...atop a pedestal. The ball on the clock is 117 feet from the lower platform. Here it is framed by some of the trees that grace the Town Clock Plaza. In addition to trees and benches, a spraying fountain and kiosks adorn the new downtown Dubuque.

Five

1981–2000

Dubuquers gather around the time capsule that was buried in 1976 for the Bicentennial of the United States. The capsule will not be opened until 2076. Photographer James L. Shaffer shot several rolls of film, slipping them in just before the lid was sealed. Someone, one hundred years from then, will have fun developing pictures of the activity surrounding the burial of the time capsule. The first eight photos in Chapter Five are memories of times gone by, and are examples of what might have gone into the time capsule.

There are a minimum of eight parades in Dubuque every year, plus any special occasions such as the 200th birthday of the United States.

Here is a stage show for an event, the Dubuque Summerfest, which is only one of many.

A Dixieland Jazz band, Dick Dodge and His All Stars, entertain the crowd while the clarinetist plays a solo at 1964's Dubuque Summerfest.

The queen candidates for the 1964 Dubuque Fest sit anxiously at the Fourth Street Ball Park, waiting for the judge's decision.

Dubuque showed the world how to throw a 100th birthday party for the State of Iowa in 1946. There were carnivals all around the city, plus parades and the crowning of a queen. All of the young ladies above hoped to wear that crown. Schools were even closed to celebrate. It worked so well that there was another held in 1947, but on a lesser scale.

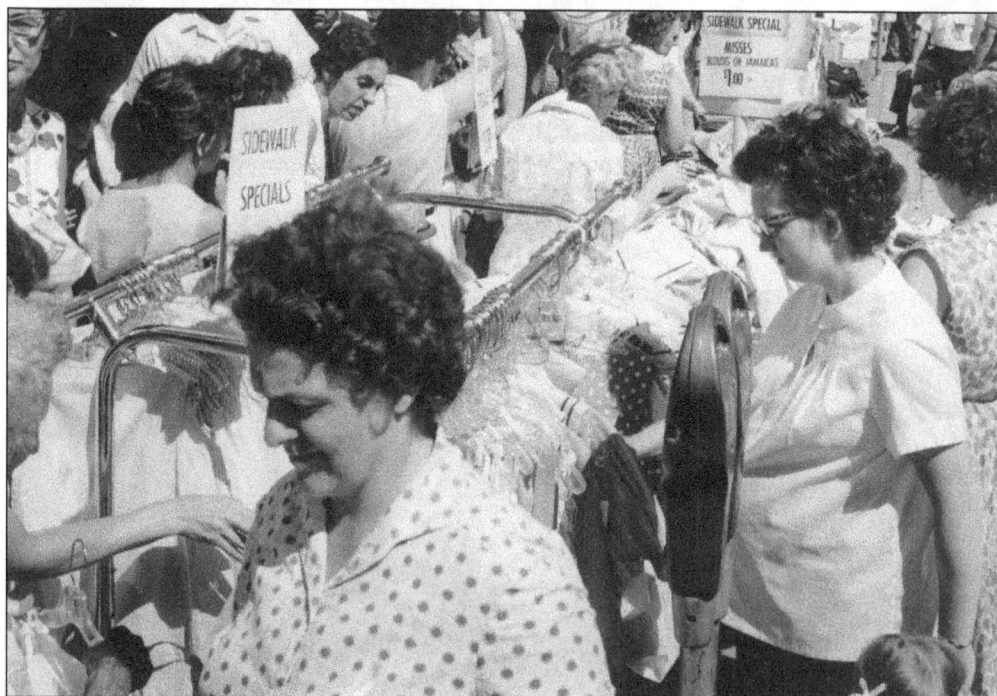

Merchants usually had their own big "shindig" during Summerfest, and would hold sidewalk sales of merchandise of every imaginable type. The above photo is from the 1964 Summerfest.

104

Remember when a person could pick up the phone and talk to a real, live operator? There were no menus from which to choose, and if a long distance call was busy or went unanswered, the operator would call you back when she made the connection. The above picture was taken in 1965 at Dubuque's Northwestern Bell Telephone Company.

Dubuquers showed their feelings when the Strand Theatre, the former Main Street Baptist Church, started exhibiting X-rated movies to survive. Survive, the theatre did not. It instead burned some time after this photo was taken. Today, a parking lot holds sway over the old site of the church-turned-theatre.

The Dubuque Star Brewery was the setting for the movie *Take This Job and Shove It*. Many local people appeared in crowd scenes, and some had speaking roles. Dubuque also hosted the stars of *F.I.S.T.* and *Field of Dreams*. Opening scenes of *Pajama Game*, written by Dubuquer Richard Bissell, were also shot in Dubuque.

The gazebo in Washington Park is a steel, three-quarters scale replica of the original structure built in 1877. One hundred years later, the Dubuque Jaycees coordinated a $57,000 Washington Park restoration. Many wedding pictures are taken at the gazebo, and some concerts provided by the local musician union and sponsored by the First National Bank were presented while office workers ate their lunches.

When Steffens Hall was found deteriorating and beyond repair it was replaced by Blades' Hall on the left, and the Jackaline Baldwin Dunlap Technology Center was added a while later. The pillared and arched wall was left standing from Steffens Hall.

Even though it burned in 1965, the State Theatre is a grim reminder of past fires in Dubuque. The Standard Lumber Company was burned in 1911, and the Canfield Hotel's older section burned in 1946 with much loss of life, including that of William Canfield and his wife, the owners. Fire can happen at any time...

...the way it did on May 17, 1984, when several of Clarke College's buildings burned. Here, flames and smoke billow from the top two floors of one of the buildings.

Clarke's chapel was beyond repair after the fire had been extinguished. The most remarkable aspect of the conflagration was the effort put forth to save the books from the library, located beneath the chapel. The books were entirely water-soaked, and appeared to be lost. Almost every refrigerator truck in the city rushed to the college, and a chain of human volunteers passed the wet books to the trucks, where they were frozen. After thawing, the majority of the books were saved.

Clarke College rebounded, and beautiful new buildings replaced the 19th century structures, which are evident in the picture above.

Once the Wisconsin High Bridge was replaced by the new Dubuque-Wisconsin Bridge, the old one was disassembled. An imaginative entrepreneur had a restaurant constructed on the limestone abutment. Using the slogan "Best Restaurant by a Dam Site," a reference to Lock and Dam Number 11, which is in plain view of the diners, tourists flock to eat there.

When Parviz Mahmoud retired from the post of conductor and music director of the Dubuque Symphony Orchestra in 1985, auditions were held the next season, and Nicholas Palmer took charge of the orchestra in 1986.

In 1980, the Dubuque Historical Society became owners of the *Wm. M. Black*, a dredge once used to keep channels open on the Missouri River. A side-wheeler, one of the paddle wheels is on display near the Riverboat Museum and Historical Complex. To give the reader an idea of the size of the paddle wheels, the empty splash guard was converted to a theatre where slide shows were held and movies of the river were run.

110

Governor Terry Branstad of Iowa, one of the two Gordons who produced *Field of Dreams*, two Chamber of Commerce officials, and Sue Riedel of Dubuque, casting director and coordinator for the final scene in that movie, announce that filming will begin in the summer of 1988.

Proceeds from the world premier of *Field of Dreams*, which starred Kevin Costner, James Earl Jones, Burt Lancaster, and Amy Madigan, went to Motion Picture Arts in Iowa. The movie was nominated for Best Picture at the Academy Awards.

The Dubuque Greyhound Park was Iowa's first greyhound racing track. Built on Chaplain Schmitt Memorial Island, formerly City Island, it had its highest handle in 1988 when it topped $66 million.

From inside the glass-enclosed stands, bettors and spectators can enjoy the races, and have lunch and libations in air-conditioned comfort.

Although the picture was taken in 1925 on Peru Road in Dubuque, the vivid memories of those who witnessed it, and also people of good will, winced when two white youths burned several crosses at African-American homes. Troublemakers from the south, one calling himself a reverend, tried to stir the pot but failed. The two white youths were sentenced to jail in the 1980s.

The miniature replica of the Statue of Liberty was more to the liking of most Dubuquers. While the KKK hides its hatred behind the American flag, the above displays Dubuquers' open love of freedom.

Menard's Home Improvement and Lumber Yard opened in 1989, further expanding Dubuque's growing west side.

Dubuque's Law Enforcement Center for both city and county is located across Central Avenue from the Dubuque County Courthouse. The Courthouse is the only example of Beaux Arts architecture in the city.

114

Pictured here is a view of Dubuque's Industrial Development on what had once been sandy soil and weeds. Beyond the trees, with the Dubuque Yacht Basin on the left, manufacturing buildings, UPS, McGraw Hill Publishers, and other businesses line Kerper Boulevard.

The Mathias Ham home today is owned by the Dubuque County Historical Society. A Fourth of July ice cream social is held each year with live music, and tours of the restored interior are conducted.

Dodge Avenue, with its sharp curves, had been a thorn in every Dubuquer's side for years. When it was rebuilt as a divided, four-lane road through town with access ramps and frontage roads, traffic flowed a lot more smoothly. Carey Lewis, an Iowa Department of Transportation engineer, oversaw the entire construction phase.

While there had been at one time as many as seven to eleven tracks to cross at Fourth, Third, and Second Streets, the redevelopment of downtown Dubuque had but two crossings and only three tracks. The switch at the right leads to the third track.

116

An elevated four-lane road takes Highways 151 and 61 to the new Dubuque-Wisconsin Bridge, which crosses the Mississippi River.

The Dubuque-Wisconsin Bridge resembles several other bridges that have been built in the last 30 years or so. Dubuque's "cookie cutter" bridge is simple in design, but not a prize winner like the Julien Dubuque Bridge.

Dubuque, Iowa's Welcome Center and Mississippi River Museum, the latter filling the upper level, was completed in 1990. A restaurant, bar, rest area, and souvenir shops abound on the first floor. The entrance to the *Diamond Jo* Gambling Casino is through the Welcome Center. Nearby, tourists and visitors can peruse the National River Hall of Fame, the Fred W. Woodward Riverboat Museum, and the *Wm. M. Black*, the huge dredge, which is permanently docked in Ice Harbor.

The *Wm. M. Black*, a sand dredge, kept the channels of the Missouri open for years. Male mannequins dressed like river men are located strategically around the boat. Tours are available to see what life on the river was like.

The *Diamond Jo* Casino is named for Joseph Reynolds, who began building his own riverboats when he felt that he was being treated unfairly by river shippers. His line, the Diamond Jo Lines, lives on in the *Diamond Jo* Casino. Notice the diamond shape between the dice on the side-wheel splash guard. At night, the casino is lighted and makes a stunning sight.

The starboard side of the *Diamond Jo* is seen here. She looks like a regular river boat, but inside is a totally different world.

Loras College's Alumni Center was completed in 1992 by Dubuque's Conlon Construction Company. Four stories tall, the fourth floor can be entered at ground level. Because it is built on the side of a bluff, the first floor also enters at ground level. A huge meeting hall/dining room/ ballroom makes up the interior, along with a computer center and small meeting/classrooms. A pub is on the third level along with a state-of-the-art kitchen and student dining area.

Upon a quick return trip to Main Street, it looks as if urban renewal is back. The Merchant's Hotel and its two adjoining buildings have been razed on the right to house the Chamber of Commerce in a building designed to blend in with its neighbors. The buildings across the street, in equally bad shape, have been razed to provide parking.

The Walsh Store moved to Dubuque in 1957, when their store in Tennyson, Wisconsin burned. It bought out the Genz Store, and in time purchased the balance of the block of buildings. The owners also opened a Tru Value Hardware Store across the alley on Iowa Street. The windows are all blanked out on the second and third floors. The cupola showing on the building's roof on the left side is actually on the roof of City Hall.

The interior of Walsh's Store shows light traffic, but the cars outside the store seem to indicate the store might just have opened. Walsh's remained closed on Sunday for years, bringing to mind a time when most stores did the same.

The Dubuque Arboretum and Botanical Garden is one of the more worthwhile attractions in Dubuque. If a stranger saw it and nothing more, that person would be overwhelmed by beauty, flowers, and overall design. The gardens are open 12 months a year.

Harold L. Shaffer and Jackson "Mac" Marshall, the Dubuque benefactor who donated 51 acres of hills and woods north of the city, belt out an old ditty to Shaffer's banjo accompaniment. The land Marshall gave became Dubuque's Arboretum and Botanical Gardens.

Another view of the Arboretum and Gardens, which are maintained by the Dubuque Arboretum Association, is shown here. Many volunteers are part of the "Adopt-A-Garden" program wherein one or more are responsible for the maintenance of a particular display. There is a visitor's center and gift ship operated by unpaid staff members. Mac's generosity was apparently contagious.

The award-winning Julien Dubuque Bridge spans the background of the Ice Harbor. One of the resident tugboats leaves the Ice Harbor through the gates in the flood wall, probably to shunt some barges from an industry to the staging area south of Dubuque.

Ah, to be a school kid again, and have nothing to look forward to but swimming and bike riding. Sutton Pool, which is near the Mississippi River, looks inviting.

Another soon-to-be swimmer slides the slide. The pool was named for Nick Sutton, a long-time recreational director for Dubuque.

Mention has been made that Dubuque is rapidly expanding to the west side. Asbury, a small village for years, has been inundated by young families building homes and has become a bedroom community. The same expansion is spreading south of Dubuque. Above is the Asbury Park.

Wal-Mart firmly established itself on the west side, and it is a rare occasion not to see the parking lot close to capacity.

Lowe's Home Improvement Center settled across Highway 20 from Menard's similar business in 1996. Business is good in Dubuque.

Medical Associates built a bigger and better clinic than they had before, when their third facility was completed. Although it appears isolated, there are quite a few restaurants, a furniture store, and at least one motel nearby.

Cartegraph Systems Inc.'s new building on Digital Drive is located on the south side of Dubuque, a rapidly-growing area. Restaurants, quick service stores, motels, and gas stations abound, as well as new homes.

When Nicholas Palmer announced his resignation as conductor and musical director of the Dubuque Symphony Orchestra in 1998, the 1999–2000 season was used to audition potential conductors to fill the position. William Intriligator was chosen and began his duties as the fifth conductor of Iowa's oldest symphony orchestra.

Because the city's namesake, Julien Dubuque, was featured in *Images of America, Dubuque, Iowa: The 19th Century*, it seems only fitting that his grave monument should close *Dubuque, Iowa: The 20th Century*. The young man seems to be looking forward to the year 2001 and the beginning of the third millennium.

ACKNOWLEDGMENTS

Carla Hines, Shaffer Photography; Center of History, Loras College; Dubuque Chamber of Commerce; Dubuque Symphony Orchestra; James L. Shaffer Collection; Joe "Kayo" Wareham; John T. Tigges Collection; Kathryn E. Tigges, typist/proofreader; Port of Dubuque River Museum.

www.ingramcontent.com/pod-product-compliance
Lightning Source LLC
Chambersburg PA
CBHW080855100426

42812CB00007B/2035